Homosexuality

Speaking the Truth in Love

Resources for Changing Lives

A Ministry of
THE CHRISTIAN COUNSELING AND
EDUCATIONAL FOUNDATION
Glenside, Pennsylvania

RCL Ministry Booklets
Susan Lutz, Series Editor

Homosexuality

Speaking the Truth in Love

Edward T. Welch

P&R PUBLISHING
P.O. BOX 817 • PHILLIPSBURG • NEW JERSEY 08865-0817

Homosexuality[1] is *the* hot issue of the day. Even more than abortion, it will confront the church throughout this generation, forcing us to listen, study, and respond wisely.

So get ready. Don't rely on your biblical study on homosexuality from a few years ago. Don't assume that knowing the criticisms of biological research on homosexuality means that you are prepared. Today new interpretations of Scripture and sophisticated medical studies are persuading more people that committed homosexual relationships are biblically permissible.

In response either we must repent and say that we have misinterpreted Scripture or we must offer a position that is compassionate, biblically sound, and able to account for the observations of current research. Also, if we maintain that homosexuality is sin, then we must not only *defend* that position, but we must develop a strategy to *pursue* homosexuals and urge them to repentance and faith.

We can defend our views through careful, prayerful study. Pursuit, however, is not easy.

We as the church must consider not only *what* we say but *how* we say it.

The *How* of Biblical Dialogue

The *how* of biblical dialogue begins with our own personal repentance. Before we confront sin in others, Matthew 7:1–5 urges us to acknowledge that the sin in our own hearts is on an even grander scale. When we do this sincerely, it can be disarming. It is hard to argue with someone who is spiritually humble! Yet, sadly, the practice is difficult and uncommon.

Many Christians can admit that they are sinners, but they don't see their sin in the same category as homosexuality. Homosexuality, being a sin "against nature" (see Rom. 1:26–27), is viewed as abnormal even among sins. Christians can see in their hearts the seed of most other sins, but many cannot even imagine being tempted by homosexuality. Yet Scripture makes it clear that homosexuality comes from the same heart that generates greed, envy, strife, disobedience to parents, and gossip (Rom. 1:29–32). As Christians, we should pursue homosexuals with humility, repentance, and not a hint of self-righteousness.

This personal repentance, however, is just the beginning. Because of our unity with the Christian church as a whole, there are corporate sins in which we share. Has the church been, at times, self-righteous toward homosexuals? Is there "homophobia" in some of our congregations, fear, or even hatred? Do we tend to think of homosexuality as worse than the gossip and private idolatries that are rampant in the church? Has the church been unwelcoming to spiritually searching homosexuals? The answer to these questions is certainly, "Yes, *we* have sinned."[2]

But what if you personally have not sinned against a homosexual? Perhaps you have never even met one. According to Daniel and Nehemiah, we may not be personally guilty for certain sins, but our unity with God's people means that we share in the church's corporate sins, and it is appropriate to confess them. Consider Daniel's prayer:

> O Lord, the great and awesome God, who keeps his covenant of love with all who love him and obey his commands, we have sinned and done wrong. We have been wicked and have rebelled; we have turned away from your commands and laws. We have not listened to your servants the prophets. . . . (Dan. 9:4–6)

This can be a starting point in speaking with homosexuals. Ask how *the church* has sinned against them. Then, if you find even a kernel of truth in what is said, ask forgiveness, and invite them to talk with you further.

If discussion seems possible, get ready for a challenging dialogue. You will be going to a place where assumptions give different meanings to words, and strategies for biblical interpretation seem completely foreign. Homosexuals have their own identity, culture, socialization process, and theories of knowledge. What seems biblically straightforward to many Christians might be understood very differently by a homosexual. Fundamental words such as "sin" may mean one thing to you but something else to homosexuals. For you it means disobedience before the Lord; for the homosexual it may mean harming other people. You appeal to the Bible as the final word in all discussion; the homosexual may appeal to feelings and certain personal and political rights. Such differences are bound to lead to misunderstanding unless we are prepared.

At the outset, the church must be clear that, although it can err in its interpretation of the Bible and is happy to be corrected, it stands under the Word of God. It cannot give away any ground on the authority of Scripture. God's Word is not always easy to apply, but we should expect the Holy Spirit to help us reach unity with those who truly want to know what God says about this important subject. The goal is discovering "Thus says the Lord."[3] Our beliefs are not rooted in our feelings; rather, they are found in the teaching of Scripture.

The Biblical Data

Even with the different grids we use, it is fairly easy to agree with homosexuals on one point: the Bible is unambiguous and consistent in prohibiting homosexuality. At every mention[4] it is condemned as sin.

> Do not lie with a man as one lies with a woman. (Lev. 18:22)

> If a man lies with a man as one lies with a woman, both of them have done what is detestable. They must be put to death; their blood will be on their own heads. (Lev. 20:13)

> Because of this [idolatry], God gave them over to shameful lusts. Even their women exchanged natural relations for unnatural ones. In the same way the men also abandoned natural relations with women and were inflamed with lust for one another. (Rom. 1:26–27)

Do not be deceived: Neither the sexually immoral nor idolaters nor adulterers nor male prostitutes nor homosexual offenders [*arsenokoitai*] . . . will inherit the kingdom of God. (1 Cor. 6:9–10)

Some argue that because Jesus did not specifically condemn homosexuality, the case against it is less conclusive. But there are many sexual behaviors that Jesus did not address specifically, such as incest, bestiality, and rape. That doesn't mean they were permissible. Jesus upheld the Old Testament law. Furthermore, he indicated that the only alternative to heterosexual marriage was celibacy (Matt. 19:10).

The Homosexual Response

Even so, the response of most homosexuals to these passages tends to be, "What does this have to do with me?" The passages are considered irrelevant because the homosexual hermeneutic (principles of interpretation) suggests that these verses refer to those who participate in "unnatural," noncommitted sexual relationships. The prohibitions, they say, do not apply to committed, loving relationships.

The reasoning goes like this: The Bible does not speak about "natural" homosexuality, only the "unnatural" cultic male prostitution or "unnatural" homosexuality practiced by heterosexually oriented people.[5] The Bible (it is argued) does not speak specifically to people who are oriented toward homosexuality.

Therefore, to develop a biblical theology of homosexuality, the homosexual hermeneutic says that we should look at other, more relevant Scripture—the texts that teach about heterosexual relationships. If the biblical principle is that sexual behavior is the privilege of committed, loving relationships, for heterosexuals it will occur within marriage; for homosexuals lacking the legal sanction of marriage, it will occur only when there is love for or loyalty to the same-sex partner. Casual homosexual or heterosexual relationships are wrong, but sex within marriage or a marriage-like relationship is good.

There are variations on this logic, but the homosexual hermeneutic is consistent on two points: (1) There is a "natural" homosexual orientation that is not addressed in Scripture, and (2) the biblical prohibitions against homosexuality do not apply to modern homosexual "marriages."

How Should We Think Biblically?

To many Christians, this sounds like a drinker who claims that the biblical passages on drunkenness do not apply to him because he is an alcoholic. But the logic cannot be discarded too quickly. Doesn't it seem that many homosexuals don't choose homosexuality? Instead, they have the orientation from birth? And isn't it true that there are differences between biblical times and now? Don't we consider some biblical passages to be time-limited cultural applications of truth rather than eternal moral verities?

For example, many churches do not require women to wear a head covering or be silent. Why? Because the Corinthian church was part of a unique culture that had distinct ways of expressing submission (1 Cor. 11:3–16). The principle is submission, not coverings. But if we can do this with coverings, why not homosexuality?

Was biblical homosexuality "unnatural," and is present homosexuality "natural"?

Current arguments rely heavily on the idea that modern homosexuality is "natural," a God-given orientation like left-handedness. The "shameful lusts" mentioned in Romans 1:26 refer to reckless homosexuality or homosexual behavior by a heterosexual.

This argument is essential to the homosexual position: homosexuality is an identity. Nobody chooses it. It just is. Homosexuality is as natural to homosexuals as heterosexuality is to heterosexuals. And how can we as Christians expect people to change their identity? How can *God* expect those *he* has oriented toward homosexuality to go against their nature?

Although most Christians don't condone homosexual activity, they have been affected by the homosexual agenda enough to believe that there is some sort of homosexual orientation. The Ramsey Colloquium, a group of Jewish and Christian scholars, certainly agree.

> Although we are equal before God, we are not born equal in terms of our strengths and weaknesses, our tendencies and dispositions, our nature and nurture. We cannot utterly change the hand we have been dealt by inheritance and family circumstances, but we are responsible for how we play that hand.[6]

Even well-known evangelicals like Tony Campolo have been sympathetic to this idea.[7] But we must be very careful at this point because the consequences are profound. For example, if you accept the idea of a sinless homosexual orientation, you will soon ask how God can hold people responsible for a homosexuality they never chose. Isn't homosexuality God's decision? The church cannot live with the idea of a natural homosexual orientation without, at some point, reinterpreting Scripture to bring it in line with our sense of the character of God. The very least that will happen is that the church will back away from the severe warnings of Scripture, such as that "homosexual offenders" will not "inherit the kingdom of God" (1 Cor. 6:9–10). This sounds too harsh for broken people who need healing (in contrast with sinners who need repentance).

A second result of accepting a homosexual orientation (while rejecting the behavior) is that all we can say to those with a homosexual orientation is "look but don't touch." "You will always think about it and want it, but don't actually *do* homosexual behavior." The victims of such counsel will never have the privilege of rooting out sin at the level of the imagination. Eventually they will feel justified in being angry with God for giving them an orientation but refusing to let them act on it.

The church must educate itself on this critical issue, so that it can engage the homosexual community in biblical discussion. The problem, however, is that the idea of homosexual orientation relies on neither biblical data nor medical research. Instead, it is a political position intended to gain homosexual rights, and it is rooted in personal experience. Therefore, neither biblical data nor critiques of the medical literature will be persuasive.

Ultimately, most homosexuals simply appeal to both their own feelings and the experience of their homosexual brothers and sisters. "Homosexuality feels right to us, so it is natural. It is part of our created constitution." Despite this potential unresponsiveness, however, we should keep examining the arguments biblically.

It is biblically possible that some Old Testament passages on homosexuality were intended, in part, to distance the Israelites from the practices of the Canaanites. One of those practices may have been the male prostitution of Canaanite religion (Deut. 23:17–18). This "unnatural" homosexuality was condemned. But is this the *only* kind of homosexual activity that is condemned?

If the Old Testament prohibitions pertained only to cultic prostitution, why would the New Testament continue them? The New Testament church did not have to distance itself from Canaanite religions. The church did, however, want to demonstrate God's holiness in its sexual behavior to distance itself from the general licentiousness of the culture.

If Leviticus were solely concerned with male prostitution, it would be a unique departure from the other biblical sexual standards.

Many Levitical laws were similar to those of the surrounding nations, but the Israelite codes consistently were morally stronger and more refined. For example, unchastity was punished more severely, and prostitution was illegal, not just regulated. Given the generally negative attitudes toward homosexual acts common in places such as Egypt, Assyria, and Babylon,[8] it would be completely out of character for the Old Testament law to prohibit homosexuality associated with idol worship while permitting it for other purposes. Even if a passage like Leviticus 18:22 did have cultic prostitution in mind, this connection would make homosexuality in general all the more abhorrent.[9]

What about the other use of "unnatural"? Is it possible that the biblical texts were referring to "unnatural" homosexual acts by heterosexuals? This would suggest that the practicing homosexuals of the Bible were involved in homosexuality against their natural design. Yet the nature of sin is that people sin because they *want* to sin (James 1:13–15). It comes from our desires. No one goes into sin kicking and screaming. Homosexuality existed in biblical times because people enjoyed it; they were oriented toward it by their own hearts (Mark 7:21–23). To make an artificial distinction between homosexual prac-

Scripture simply did not know of committed homosexual relationships?" After all, the prejudice against homosexuality was intense, leaving homosexuals little opportunity for committed relationships.

Such an argument suggests that the Old Testament was naive about sexual relations, but a quick reading of Leviticus 18–20 suggests otherwise. Details of the sexual practices of Old Testament times are unclear, but the sheer number of prohibitions suggests that a wide range of sexual possibilities was well known. What's more, the sexual practices of New Testament times are better known to us, and it is certain that the Greek and Roman cultures had every kind of homosexuality imaginable. Yet the apostle Paul suggests no exceptions to the prohibitions against homosexuality.

It is true that, on some level, there can be great affection and commitment in homosexual relationships. But this doesn't mean that God approves of them. A man may be unbiblically divorced to marry a woman he believes he truly loves, yet this union would still be wrong. Adulterous relationships may be, on some level, "loving and committed," but they are still wrong.

With this point many homosexuals may agree. Someone, namely the nonadulterous spouse, is being victimized by the adultery. But what about love and loyalty when no one else seems to be hurt? Such an argument does not understand biblical love. Love is not simply the absence of obvious injury to anyone. For example, critical thoughts don't victimize, but they are wrong. To limit love to such definitions completely misses the biblical teaching.

Love is understood not by our definition but by God's. It is defined as obedience toward God. We do not independently decide what form love takes. God tells us how to love. When we love on *our* terms rather than God's, we are in sin. Even if our sin does not seem to be hurting anyone, it is still sin. If sin were reduced to hurting others, then we could become morally perfect by isolating ourselves from all people. Sin, however, is not primarily a human-against-human action. It is human-against-God.

Are the biblical prohibitions against homosexuality part of the obsolete Old Testament ceremonial codes?

Another objection raised by homosexuals is that these Levitical prohibitions are ceremonial, enforced only during a specific period in Israel's history. Like the laws declaring certain animals unclean, the laws against homosexuality are no longer applicable.

There are two reasons why this argument does not hold up. First, the penalty for violation was death. This was the penalty for moral violations rather than violations of ceremonial law. Second, the New Testament writers considered the laws to be applicable.

Are the prohibitions against homosexuality an application of the command to fill the earth, which is no longer relevant in a heavily populated world?

A fourth objection is that the command against homosexuality was written to a culture that felt the mandate to fill the earth and subdue it. Homosexuality, because it is sterile, would not be politically correct in such an environment. With the coming of Christ, some suggest, the mandate was rightly interpreted as a command to evangelize—a spiritual filling more than a reproductive one. Furthermore, in an overpopulated world, we no longer need to emphasize procreation.

This may seem like grasping at straws at first, but parts of the argument would probably be acceptable to most Christians. For instance, how many people use birth control? Doesn't this violate the commandment to fill the earth? Or what about marriages that choose to be childless? Are such people excommunicated? How is a homosexual union different from a heterosexual union that is barren or chooses to be childless?

The homosexual argument would have some merit if the purpose of marriage were simply to reproduce. But marriage is a covenant of companionship ordained by God. It brings together as one flesh two people who are truly "fit" for each other. It is not deficient or immoral when the marriage is barren, but it is immoral if there is a violation of the marital design.

This takes us back again to the validity of committed, loving, homosexual relationships. Aren't these covenants of companionship? Why can't two loving people of the same sex enjoy the privilege of marital sexuality? Again, God defines the way we love each other.

The Biblical Position

Before leaving this brief biblical discussion, let's remember that we all can find ways to use Scripture to support our views. Our hearts enjoy sin and are quick to self-justify and self-deceive. Is it possible we are self-deceived in our use of Scripture because we find homosexuality threatening and different? It is possible. Our response is to prayerfully search our own hearts and prayerfully approach Scripture. This, I trust, is what we have done.

Is it also possible that homosexuals are self-deceived because they want their own desires more than obedience to God? Is it possible that, like good defense lawyers, they try to plant a seed of doubt so they can liberate their consciences and practice their desires? This possibility should be seriously considered because the homosexual argument disagrees with a plain reading of Scripture, contradicts the history of biblical interpretation, and is reminiscent of the Pharisaic narrowing of the law so prevalent in the New Testament.

The Bible teaches that there is a creation order for human sexuality. God's ordained design for sexual relationships is male-female. Homosexual *acts* and homosexual *desire*, by either male or female, are a violation of this creation ordinance and are thus sinful. This being so, the church must warn and rebuke those who call themselves Christians but persist in homosexual practice, *and* the church must actively teach that homosexual affection is sinful. There is no morally neutral, in-born, homosexual orientation. To tell those struggling with homosexual desire to simply refrain from acting on it is to sin against these brothers and sisters.

Biological Causes

Biological research has been used to support the theory of a predestined homosexual orientation—the idea that homosexuality is part of our biological make-up, not our sin nature. But since Scripture consistently teaches that homosexuality is an expression of a sinful heart, we should expect certain results in the scientific literature. Negatively, we should expect that science will not be able to establish a biological cause to homosexuality. Positively, we should expect science to be friendly with the biblical position. And this, indeed, is the case: the findings of science support rather than challenge the biblical view.

Perhaps the most well known study on the biology of homosexuality appeared in the periodical *Science*.[10] The lead researcher, Simon LeVay, conducted post-mortem examinations on the brains of nineteen homosexual men who died from AIDS and sixteen presumed heterosexual men, six of whom died of AIDS.

His results suggested that the brains of the heterosexual men consistently had more brain cells in a specific area of the brain (INAH 3) believed to be involved in sexual behavior. When this data is interpreted with a homosexuality-as-biologically-determined bias, the conclusion is that homosexuality is located in the brain.

But Christians and non-Christians have frequently noted that the results of this study do not establish a causative link between brain activity and homosexual behavior. Even LeVay recognizes the limitations of his study, suggesting that it is little more than an invitation to further research. He knows that his observations are tentative until confirmed by other researchers, and this corroboration has not as yet been forthcoming. He recognizes that AIDS may have confounded the results, that the sample size was too small to draw any clear conclusions, and that his measurements could be prone to error. Furthermore, the brains of three homosexual men in the study were indistinguishable from the analogous brain areas in heterosexual men. Even his assumption that there is a relationship between INAH 3 and sexual behavior has never been clearly established.

The conclusion, therefore, is that we can conclude nothing from this study. *Science* even published a letter to the editor criticizing the journal for prematurely publishing an article of dubious quality.[11]

Yet let's say that, eventually, research that avoids the weaknesses of this study actually established a connection between the size of INAH 3 and homosexuality. Even then, LeVay acknowledged that "the results do not allow one to decide if the size of INAH 3 in an individual is the cause or the consequence of that individual's sexual orientation." In other words, from his perspective it may be just as likely that the possible brain differences are a *result* of homosexuality rather than a cause.[12]

Or let's take the most extreme (and currently hypothetical) possibility. Let's suggest that someone could demonstrate that INAH 3 is, indeed, a participant in sexual desire and that INAH 3 is smaller *from birth* in people who eventually become homosexuals. In other words, the brain is not laying down neuronal patterns that are a *result* of homosexual experience. Instead, the smaller INAH 3 is apparent *before* any homosexual activity.

If such research were to exist, Christians and many non-Christians would make at least the following observations. First, there would always be exceptions to the rule. Some heterosexuals would have a smaller INAH 3 and some homosexuals would have a large INAH 3. Second, even the secular writers would be firm in saying, as they are now, that biology is not destiny. Human sexual response is too complex to reduce to a deficit of neurons in the brain. Third, Christians would remain firm in their view that biology can't make us sin. At most, biology is analogous to a friend who tempts us into sin. In such cases the friend might be a trial, but the friend can be rebuked and resisted.[13]

Another area of biological research explores the occurrence of homosexuality in families and twins. It attempts to uncover a genetic tendency to the behavior. A frequently cited example of such research was done by Michael Bailey and Richard Pillard.[14] Their study reported that of fifty-six homosexual men who were identical twins, 52 percent (twenty-nine) had a twin brother who was also homosexual. Among nonidentical twins the rate was 22 percent; among nontwin brothers the rate was 9 percent; and among adopted siblings the rate was 11 percent. The research group also found comparable statistics with females.[15]

This is what you would expect if there was a genetic component to homosexuality: the closer the genetic relationship, the higher the rate of shared homosexuality.

To be blunt, while interesting, this study is meaningless. Even if you ignore the sampling biases (subjects were recruited through homosexual publications) and the fact that no other researchers have found such high percentages among identical twins, the study is inconsequential. This is because identical twins typically have a profound influence on each other. If one twin is introduced to something new, it is likely that he will introduce the other twin to that activity. Also, why did genetically unrelated, adopted brothers of homosexuals have such an allegedly high rate of homosexuality? Their 11 percent incidence rate was five times what you would expect. (The incidence rate of active homosexuality is generally believed to be about 2 percent in the general population.)[16] The study would be better used to support the influence of peers in the development of homosexuality.

The researchers are aware that the only thing they really proved is that homosexuality is *not* solely caused by genetics. If genetics were the only contributor to homosexual activity, then the concordance rate in identical twins would be 100 percent. If one twin were homosexual, the other twin would *always* be homosexual. Since the statistic is much lower than that, homosexuality cannot be a straightforward genetic trait. Apart from this conclusion, the study is not able to prove anything. Along with problems in the way the study was structured, identical twins share an environment that is more similar than that of other siblings. Therefore, it is not unusual for them to share sins. The only way to strengthen this research would be to study twins who were separated at birth.

But let's again suppose that this research were supported by better studies. What if research found that identical twins more frequently share homosexuality even when they have no contact with each other?

If this research were to emerge, it would still illustrate biblical truth. First, there would never be a 100-percent concordance rate. Second, a principle of Scripture is that the context for our lives is the physical body, so we should expect that the physical body (the brain in this case) would have some way to biologically represent what is happening in the heart. It is even possible that a certain brain type is necessary to express homosexual intent. This brain or genetic hardware is not enough in itself to cause homosexuality (that is, it may not be *sufficient*), but it may need to be present if homosexuality is to emerge (that is, it may be *necessary*). To put it another way, a certain genetic predisposition may be necessary (an essential element) for homosexual intent, but it is not determinative—its presence does not force you to be homosexual.

It is important to be precise in making this point. Am I suggesting that it is biblically possible that the body could cause homosexuality? In a way, I am, but I am using the word "cause" to mean "biologically shape or influence," not "irresistibly compel." Used this way, there is nothing shocking about the statement. It is simply saying that the way our sinful hearts are actually expressed in behavior is the result of hundreds of factors, biology being one. A person whose sinful heart is expressed in murder may have been influenced by unjust treatment, parents who allowed him to abuse his siblings, and Satan's encouragements to kill. But none of these influences remove personal responsibility. The ultimate cause of sin is always the sinful heart.

A third type of biological research on homosexuality focuses on genetic data at the microscopic level, on the gene itself. The best known of the research teams doing this work is from the National Institute of Health and is headed by Dean Hamer.[17] This highly technical work is relatively new, but neither its youth nor its sophistication should keep the Christian lay person from asserting the functional authority of Scripture over the data.

Like the two studies previously mentioned, there are methodological flaws in this study. It has not been duplicated, so very little can be said at this point. Also, even if practicing homosexuals were consistently genetically distinct from heterosexuals, this would not make homosexuality a biologically based behavior for which people are not morally responsible.

These three studies are the most recent in a relatively long but fruitless attempt to find a biological cause for homosexuality. A physician who reviewed the literature said, "Recent studies postulate biologic factors as the primary basis for sexual orientation. However, there is no evidence at present to substantiate a biologic theory, just as there is no evidence to support any singular psychosocial explanation."[18] The only thing certain is that human sexuality is too complex to be reduced to the workings of the brain.

Since behavior is expressed (not caused) by our biology, we should not be surprised if we hear of future studies that offer better evidence for a biology-and-behavior link. But Scripture is clear: our bodies can never make us sin. The body is weak but is not the cause of sin. This principle, when used accurately, can bring increased clarity to brain research. The brain sciences can offer exciting observations, but they can only be rightly interpreted when Scripture provides the contours.

A Biblical Model of Homosexuality

The church has been quick to refute the biological research, but it has been slow to apply the same principles to the psychological theories. For various reasons many people tend to be more comfortable with psychological influences than biological ones. Note, for example, how well *Homosexuality: A New Christian Ethic*[19] is received by many Christians. In this book Elizabeth Moberly suggests that behind almost all homosexuality, male or female, is a deficit in the relationship with the same-sex parent. The theory is that there is a God-designed need for same-sex love, affirmation, acceptance, and bonding. When these allegedly normal attachment needs have been left unmet, the needs become eroticized at puberty. Homosexuality is a drive to make good this relationship.

When we listen closely to the application of this and other psychological explanations,[20] we find good intent but a flawed understanding of the doctrine of sin. These psychological theories emphasize that homosexuality is learned rather than biologically inbred; and since it is learned, it can be unlearned.

But notice the problem. All this does is suggest that the orientation toward homosexuality starts a little later than birth instead of before birth. We are left at almost the same place as the biological theories: the orientation is still established by forces outside of ourselves, and orientation precedes sin (figure 1). Therefore, the real problem, the deep problem, is the homosexual orientation. A diagnosis of sin and a cure that included repentance would be considered superficial.

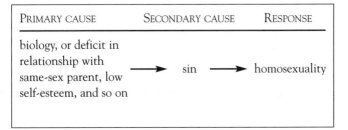

PRIMARY CAUSE	SECONDARY CAUSE	RESPONSE
biology, or deficit in relationship with same-sex parent, low self-esteem, and so on	→ sin →	homosexuality

Figure 1. A Common, Unbiblical Conceptualization of the Development of Homosexuality

PRIMARY CAUSE	SECONDARY INFLUENCES	SINFUL PRACTICE
sinful heart →	genetics, peers, family, sexual violation by an older person, and so on →	homosexuality

Figure 2. The Development of Homosexuality

A biblical view acknowledges that there may be psychological and biological influences in the development of homosexuality. In fact, the Bible would warn us not to limit the vast number of possible influences. However, Scripture is adamant that it is not what influences us that makes us "unclean." Instead, "from within, out of men's hearts, come evil thoughts, sexual immorality. . . . All these evils come from inside and make a man 'unclean' " (Mark 7:21–23) (figure 2). This means that our sinful orientation has innumerable expressions in our lives. With some it is greed or jealousy, with others it is sinful anger, and with others it can be expressed in homosexual desire.

The Process of Change

Like all sin, homosexuality at the heart level does not relent easily or quickly. It is put to death over time in the course of progressive sanctification. But change is certainly possible. "Such were some of you" (1 Cor. 6:11 NASB) is the often-repeated reminder that there is hope to overcome both homosexual acts *and* homosexual desire.

How does this happen? The way of change is familiar. You need no special techniques. It consists of simultaneously juggling two themes: the knowledge of ourselves and the knowledge of God. These themes are presented in love and with a willingness to listen.

Listening is a good place to start. After all, how can we bring truth to a person unless we know him? So you might begin with questions. What is it like for the person to struggle with homosexuality? What events shaped his or her present expression of homosexuality? Past events may need to be addressed. Was the person sexually abused or manipulated into sexual activity? This victimization doesn't explain homosexuality or excuse people for their future thoughts and actions. But God certainly speaks with compassion to those who have been sinned against, and homosexuals must hear this.

How has the person been hurt in relationships? How has it been painful to pursue a homosexual lifestyle? What is it like to face the reality of leaving close friends, long-term partners, or a supportive community? "I ached physically from all the emotional turmoil," said a man who was leaving his partner. "But several Christian heterosexual men made themselves available any time of the day or night. I'm alive today because those guys loved me."[21]

In this context we introduce the knowledge of God, especially God's forgiveness of sinners. This both attracts and changes those struggling with homosexuality. Some Christians may suggest that there is enough teaching that God warmly embraces everyone and not enough on God's hatred of sin and his justice. This may be true, but it is no reason to sacrifice the greatness of the doctrine of grace. Homosexuals are in a complex position: they are rebels against a Holy God; but they are also, at some level, aware of their sins and afraid of God's wrath (Rom. 1). They do not believe that God could really bring himself to forgive homosexuals. As C. John Miller said, "There is no more important factor in the transforming of a homosexual than confident faith that his or her sins really have been pardoned by God at their deepest root."[22]

To know the grace of forgiveness, homosexuals must know the truth about themselves: they are sinners in need of grace. Even though they have some knowledge of this, they often lack biblical clarity because their knowledge of sin is suppressed. The flesh does not want to see sin in all its ugliness; it works to keep it covered. What clouds sin even more is the myth that there is, by God's design, a homosexual orientation. These two factors work tirelessly against the truth about ourselves.

The Holy Spirit exposes our hearts through the application of Scripture. The goal is to understand what God says. The goal is to learn to "think God's thoughts." One way into the Scripture is to understand that there actually *is* something deeper than homosexuality. As summarized in Romans 1, homosexuality is an expression of an idolatrous heart. *This* is our deepest problem. We have an instinct that switches our allegiance from God to our idols. What are our idols? Comfort, pleasure, power, personal meaning, self-esteem, and so on. The possibilities are endless, but they all have one thing in common: an allegiance to self. We rebel against God, and we choose to live for our glory rather than God's. We choose to obey our own desires rather than God's Word. Homosexual desire or activity is an expression of the idolatrous instincts of our hearts.

Does the person have questions about homosexual orientation? Does he have a sense that he was always more interested in same-sex relationships? If so, stick with this issue until the person can think biblically about it. It is too easy to settle for the absence of homosexual behavior and not worry about attitudes.

Remember that it is on the question of homosexual orientation that the world, flesh, and Devil converge. The world has voted that homosexuality is normal. Our flesh wants to exonerate ourselves from homosexual fantasy. And the Devil stands behind both, whispering his murderous deceptions. The deception of homosexual orientation must be exposed and corrected. It is a false teaching that will eventually lead to bad fruit. We truly do have an "orientation," but it is a spiritual orientation that is against God. It is not a simple physical inclination.

As the Holy Spirit exposes these critical issues about the person, the Spirit also reveals more of the knowledge of God. The theme of God's love continues, but now we are reminded that it is a *holy* love. By holy we mean that it is unparalleled in human experience. It is beyond comprehension, and it is unsurpassed. As a result, it leaves witnesses in awe. This is the beginning of the fear of the Lord. When we witness his forgiveness, we learn the fear of the Lord (Ps. 130:4). When the disciples saw his power over the wind and the waves, "they were terrified" and grew in the fear of the Lord (Mark 4:41). When Isaiah was taken into the throne room, he was so overwhelmed by the holiness of God that he cried out, "I am ruined!" (Isa. 6:5). Isaiah's knowledge of God's holy majesty and forgiveness established him in the fear of the Lord for the rest of his ministry. Indeed, the fear of the Lord is both the beginning of wise living and its goal.

One of the great blessings of the fear of the Lord is that it can teach us to hate sin (Prov. 8:13). The knowledge of the holy can mobilize. It can take the drudgery out of daily self-control. It can make us warriors against the tendencies of our sinful nature. This aggressive stance toward sin is especially critical since our problem is that we *like* it. It has the power of our affections. If we don't root out these affections, we are guaranteed that temptation will always be nearly overpowering. The fear of the Lord can keep us battle-ready. With the heavenly throne in sight, we do battle with the "sin that so easily entangles" (Heb. 12:1).

> Therefore, I do not run like a man running aimlessly; I do not fight like a man beating the air. No, I beat my body and make it my slave so that after I have preached to others, I myself will not be disqualified for the prize. (1 Cor. 9:26–27)

> Let us run with perseverance the race marked out for us. Let us fix our eyes on Jesus. (Heb. 12:1–2)

What expectations should there be for change? What is the goal? The goal, again, is to think God's thoughts rather than our own. This means that we can battle when we see the very *seeds* of homosexual temptation (James 1:13–15). We can grow to hate anything that hints of rebellion against God. We can be liberated from homosexual obsession. And we can understand that male-female marriage is one of God's good gifts. This does not mean that all people who once struggled with homosexuality will pursue marriage. In some cases God gives grace to be celibate. But since marriage is a good gift, and God's pleasure is toward Christian marriage, former homosexuals whose minds and hearts are renewed will find pleasure in the same thing that God does.

How long will it take? If a person is willing to follow Christ, and is surrounded by a caring church, homosexual behavior can stop immediately. "The grace of God . . . teaches us to say 'No' to ungodliness and worldly passions, and to live self-controlled, upright and godly lives" (Titus 2:11–12).

No one should think, however, that homosexual *desire* will be gone as quickly. The person with a long history of homosexual practice will be doing battle for many years. The power of homosexual thoughts will gradually be defeated, but the stray homosexual thought may be evident decades later.

Is this discouraging? Does this mean that deliverance is necessary? No, it means that God is at work, giving power to fight, reminding us that warfare is normal, progressively sanctifying us, and giving us the privilege of constantly depending on Christ by faith.

For these goals to be reached, one-time homosexuals need more than a counselor. Like us all, they need the larger body of Christ and its varied relationships. Men need other men who love, listen, and model brotherly relationships. Women need other women with whom they can have close but not obsessive or sexualized relationships. Both men and women need godly relationships with the opposite sex and with elders and pastors who can faithfully pray and, if necessary, bring church discipline as a means of God's loving correction.

Other relationships might include small groups with couples and singles, accountability groups with other men, and small prayer groups. In some cases churches may have specialized ministries to homosexuals (e.g., support groups) or more general ministries to those who want to leave sexual slavery of any kind.

An effective church should have homosexuals! Because of the love of Christ, the church should pursue homosexuals. And through its exaltation of Christ in preaching, corporate prayer, and worship, the church should attract homosexuals. It should minister the Word to those who are already in church by flushing out the self-deceived, exposing the dishonest, confronting the rebel, offering forgiveness to the guilt-ridden, and giving hope.

The church should also welcome those who struggle with homosexuality but have never been part of the church. The church should surprise them with love, a sense of family, and the absence of self-righteous judgment. It should offer truth in a way that is convicting, attractive, and radically different from anything else the homosexual has ever heard. May God enable us to fulfill this high calling.

Endnotes

1 Homosexuality can be defined as thoughts or actions, in adult life, motivated by a definite erotic (sexual-genital-orgiastic) attraction to members of the same sex, usually but not necessarily leading to sexual relations with them. Even though there are differences between male and female homosexuality, I will use the term "homosexual" to refer to male or female, unless otherwise indicated.

2 Of course, this does not mean that we apologize for what Scripture says.

3 Oxford University professor Alister McGrath indicates rightly that we live in a time when "openness and relevance are more important than truth. This, however, is intellectual shallowness and moral irresponsibility." Michael Foucault has stated that "truth" in a post-modern world is nothing more than a compliment.

4 For example, J. Nelson, "Homosexuality and the Church: Towards a Sexual Ethics of Love," *Christianity and Crisis* 37 (1977), 63–69.

5 "Morality and Homosexuality," *The Wall Street Journal*, 24 February 1994, 3.

6 Anthony Campolo, "A Christian Sociologist Looks at Homosexuality," *The Wittenburg Door*, October-November 1977, 16–17. Also, T. Evans, "Homosexuality: Christian Ethics and Psychological Research," *Journal of Psychology and Theology*, 3 (1975), 94–98.

7 D. Sherwin Bailey, *Homosexuality and the Western Christian Tradition* (London: Longmans, Green & Co., 1995).

8 Greg Bahnsen also notes, "Parallel reasoning would lead us to deem bestiality [mentioned in Leviticus

12:23] outside of religious or cultic contexts as morally acceptable—a conclusion that ought to shock our ethical sensibilities." In *Homosexuality: A Biblical View* (Grand Rapids: Baker, 1978), 45.

9 A. Dostourian, "Gayness: A Radical Christian Approach," in L. Crew, ed., *The Gay Academic* (Palm Springs: ETC, 1978), 347.

10 Simon LeVay, "A Difference in Hypothalamic Structure Between Heterosexual and Homosexual Men," *Science* 253 (1991), 1034–37.

11 Joseph M. Carrier and George Gellert, *Science* 254 (1991), 630.

12 Another possibility is that the brain is neither cause nor result. For example, people who demonstrate sinful anger would demonstrate different patterns of brain activity than those who were very peaceful because of faith in Christ. But such an observation does not mean that the brain makes us angry. It simply means that the brain is the physical representation of the intents of the heart.

13 This analogy is also applicable to experiences such as PMS.

14 J. Michael Bailey and Richard C. Pillard, "A Genetic Study of Male Sexual Orientation," *Archives of General Psychiatry* 48 (1991), 1089–97.

15 J. Michael Bailey, Richard C. Pillard, Michael C. Neale, and Yvonne Agyei, "Heritable Factors Influence Sexual Orientation in Women," *Archives of General Psychiatry* 50 (1993), 217–24.

16 John O. Billy, Koray Tanfer, William R. Grady, and Daniel H. Klepinger, "The Sexual Behavior of Men in the United States," *Family Planning Perspectives* 25 (1993), 52–61.

17 Dean H. Hamer, Stella Hu, Victoria L. Magnuson, Nan Hu, and Angela M. Patatucci, "A Linkage Be-

tween DNA Markers on the X Chromosome and Male Sexual Orientation," *Science* 261 (1993), 321–27.

18 William Byne and Bruce Parsons, "Homosexual Orientation: The Biologic Theories Reappraised," *Archives of General Psychiatry* 50 (1993), 228–39.

19 Elizabeth Moberly, *Homosexuality: A New Christian Ethic* (Stony Point, South Carolina: Attic, 1983).

20 Others have suggested that homosexuality is a result of victimization. For example, E. Hurst and D. Jackson, *Overcoming Homosexuality* (Elgin, Illinois: David C. Cook, 1987); Leanne Payne, *A Broken Image* (Westchester, Illinois: Crossway, 1981) and *Crisis in Masculinity* (Westchester, Illinois: Crossway, 1985).

21 Bob Davies, "Will We Offer Hope?" *Moody*, May 1994, 16.

22 C. John Miller, "The Gay '80s," *Eternity*, November 1986, 18.

Edward T. Welch *is academic dean of the faculty and director of counseling at the Christian Counseling and Educational Foundation, Glenside, Pennsylvania.*